Who Says Learning Spanish Can't Be Fun?

The 3-Day Guide to Speaking Fluent Spanish

Zavier Jepson

Copyright © 2018 Zavier Jepson

Table of Contents

Introduction

Chapter 1: On Language Learning

Chapter 2: Pronunciation, Irregular Verbs, and Basic Phrases

Chapter 3: Days 7-14 - Regular Verbs: Past, Present, and Future

Chapter 4: Days 14-21 - Prepositions, Conjunctions, and Starting a Routine

Chapter 5: Days 21-30 - Building on Your Routine and Immersion

Chapter 6: The Three-Day Masterclass

Conclusion

Introduction

Congratulations on downloading *Who Says Learning Spanish Can't Be Fun?* and thank you for doing so.

The following chapters will discuss everything that you need to know to rapidly become a competent Spanish speaker in a very short time.

There are a lot of reasons that you might want to learn Spanish. Perhaps you're taking a vacation to a South American country and want to be able to speak to the natives with very little effort expended. Perhaps you're having an important business meeting with a potential client whose first language is Spanish and you want to make them feel warm, or you have to take a business trip to Argentina. Maybe you've just married into a family with a lot of Spanish speakers and you want to be able to keep up with conversations at the holidays. Regardless of your exact reasoning, you've picked up this book because you want to be able to quickly and efficiently speak Spanish.

To that end, you've picked up the perfect book. This book is ideal for you because it doesn't require you to have a lot of in-depth knowledge of languages, nor does it require you to be a "natural" language learner - it takes advantage of your brain's natural aptitude for learning language and then bends them so that you may rapidly learn Spanish and be speaking fluently in no time.

This book contains two different courses; the first is a 30-day course where you can spend roughly one hour per day at most working on your Spanish and then be a relatively fluent speaker by the end of the month. The second speeds up that into a 3-day crash course where you're going to be spending a lot more time each day, but you'll get the desired results much faster.

What does this mean? This means that on a 3-day weekend, with nothing else to do, you can come out of it speaking a language fluently. Additionally, after only 30 days you can be an amazing Spanish speaker who sounds like a natural.

There are plenty of books on this subject on the market, thanks again for choosing this one! Every effort was made to ensure it is full of as much useful information as possible, please enjoy!

Chapter 1: On Language Learning

The first thing that we've got to do is clear up a lot of misconceptions about language learning. This is important because in order for you to be successful with learning Spanish - or any language - you absolutely must think about it in the right way. Otherwise, you're going to just be wasting your own time as you scramble along confused, and you're going to forget everything that you've learned in a week or two.

In my life, I have helped a lot of people to learn additional languages. Spanish is one of the most frequent ones that I've worked with. A lot of the time, people seek language tutoring because they are frustrated with the usual avenues for learning languages. For example, they'll tell me that they simply aren't *made* for language learning, or that their brain isn't wired "that way". This, of course, is an utter lie.

The truth is that everybody is geared towards language learning. There's not a single person on Earth who can't learn a language. Our brains are actually geared towards language learning. Think about it in a natural way. The one thing that humans have uniquely - the one thing which has set us apart in such an extreme way - is the fact that we've got such a simply *intelligent* brain. The fact that we can reason and communicate is what sets us apart from other animals. We've developed in such a way that we are *absolutely* a social animal, meant to communicate with others. After all, it's what we had to do to survive!

So, your brain - and everybody's brain, for that matter - is actually hardwired towards language learning. This is most evident when a person is a child because their brain is trying extra hard to forge associations between *words* and *concepts*. And this in and of itself is an important distinction.

Take, for instance, an *apple*. When you think of an *apple*, you are thinking of a fruit that grows from an apple true. However, there is no natural rule that these things are called "apples"; in fact, if you go back only 600 years, the English word for "apple" was different. Rather, you're matching the word "apple" to the *concept* of the apple. Meanwhile, somebody who was born in France would attach the word *pomme* to the concept of an apple, and somebody born in Mexico would attach the word *manzana* to the concept of an apple. All of these things are apples, but they have different words for the same concept.

Understanding this key part of language learning is important to understand how you may *learn* a language.

See, every word is just a link to a concept. Your brain is designed to attach words to concepts, even after you're past your "prime" language learning age. The brain is most efficiently forging these connections when you're younger because it doesn't *have* words for these concepts yet. However, you can still take advantage of this when you're older.

Let me also clear up another misconception about language learning, if you do it properly, you can't learn *too many* languages. As you can probably guess from the way that the brain forges connections, the important thing is rather that you're *practicing* each language. You'll subconsciously compartmentalize each language into its own section if you learn them correctly, and there will be little overlap.

The "practicing" concept is also the reason that when somebody moves to a foreign country and has to pick up the tongue there, they can actually *lose* their mother tongue if they quit using it. After all, a language is only a collection of concepts that have been given names and a specific way of communicating those concepts, and if you're not doing this important step of *communicating* the concepts, you're going to forget them.

However, on the flip side, the more that you use a language, the more that you subconsciously start to attach these concepts to one another. This means that the longer you spend working with a language, the easier it will become to work with it as your brain will start forging connections between concepts and words on their own.

So, there's still an element we haven't talked about. What does any of this have to do with this book? And moreover, why does this mean you'll have a different experience with *this* book than you have in learning Spanish in high school?

Well, the thing that you have to understand is that the academic method for learning a language is great in terms of the academic system - it's great for giving a way to establish grades and letting a kid understand the basic concepts behind another language, and perhaps even remember how to have basic conversation in it. However, it's not great at setting a person up for *practical* usage of a language.

This method is different because it involves working with practical methods as an integral part of learning the language. Reading, speaking, listening, and writing the language will become normal parts of your daily use as you start to go through everything and build up a strong foundation.

This language learning method looks at language learning as a bit of a pyramid. You can divide a pyramid into three sections.

The bottom section is the *foundation*. These are things that allow you to communicate on the most basic level in a language. Believe it or not, did you know that you can get around in a language knowing only one verb tense and the five-hundred most common words? And the five-hundred most common words are learned extremely quickly, too. I'd wager a bit that you could even *reduce* that to 300 words and still feel pretty comfortable getting around. It's true!

These "broken" forms of languages are known as *pidgins*. There are many examples of pidgins being used. Take, for example, World War II; American troops in Italy needed to get around in the war-ravaged cities, but lacked a great background in Italian. Therefore, they learned the basics of the language, the most important words, and how to conjugate verbs in the present tense. (We'll talk more about this later, don't worry.)

The Italians were able to understand them, and they were able to get around just fine.

Being able to speak in a pidgin form of a language is the first step towards getting around in a foreign circumstance. While you certainly won't be writing any Shakespeare-level literature in the language, you'll be able to get around, which is more important to a beginner language learner anyway.

Then, on the second level, you have the *arbitrations*. These are things which build on top of the foundation and make you a bit more understood, but they aren't necessary for just getting around on a day-to-day basis. Examples of arbitrations would include things such as being able to name every single item in the grocery store or being able to fluently and flawlessly navigate different verb tenses. These are nonetheless *important*, but they aren't as important as the foundation, and they *require* the foundation in order to be used.

Then, the third level makes the *finishers*. These are the concepts which allow you to traverse high-level discussions like philosophy or politics. These typically are rather simple after you've gotten comfortable with the arbitrations because by then you're aware of the ins and outs of the language. When you're just starting out, though, these things can seem somewhat impossible.

The problem with traditional classes is that they lump them all together and just make you study endless terms and conjugations without any real reprieve for you as the student, and this method also doesn't take advantage of your natural language learning abilities.

The truth is that some memorization is going to be necessary while you learn the foundation. However, it doesn't make sense for you to learn arbitrations and finishers for things which don't *matter* to you. If I force you to memorize the word for *eggplant*, you aren't going to just *remember* it because you will hardly ever use it outside of context. Rather, the brain must *need* something in order to remember it effectively. The best course of action is to put yourself in situations where your brain *naturally* forges the concepts.

Therefore, the point of this book is to *give* you the foundation, then give you the methods by which you may *build up* the arbitrations and finishers.

If you've become disillusioned with language learning and have started to feel like there's just no avenue for you as a language learner and like you'll never start to feel comfortable working with a foreign language, then prepare to be corrected. This is one of the most effective language learning methods I've ever worked with because it puts *you* in the driver's seat.

Be forewarned, though; the nature of this requires that *you* put in the work. The thing about this method of language learning is that ultimately you are the one deciding whether you are successful or not. This means that the approach is going to be quite different from any sort of classroom setting that you've tried out before.

Chapter 2: Pronunciation, Irregular Verbs, and Basic Phrases

During this chapter, we're going to be covering the things you need to spend your first week doing. During this week, you need to be working on memorizing the different aspects of the foundation that you're trying to build. This is going to be one of the periods that deals most with raw memorization than anything else.

Fortunately, it's going to be one of the only ones. So, what are we going to be going over in this chapter, exactly?

Well, we're going to be going over the basics pertaining to Spanish so that you can start practicing your reading and speaking, as well as give you some content to practice so that you can have a basic conversation in Spanish. By the end of this chapter, you will feel relatively confident talking to a stranger and telling just a bit about yourself.

The first thing that we need to cover in this chapter is the Spanish pronunciation. Spanish pronunciation in many ways is similar to English, but there are some important ways in which it departs.

It's also important at this point that I give a disclaimer.

There are two primary dialects of Spanish, and then a few smaller distinctions within those. The two primary dialects of Spanish are *Castilian* or *Castellano*, which is spoken in Spain, and *Español*, which is spoken primarily in Latin America. Between these, there are a few differences. It's much like comparing British English to American English; pronunciation and certain words will be different, but for the most part, they are mutually intelligible.

This book is going to focus specifically upon Latin American Spanish because more people speak that version and most Americans are wanting to learn that version of Spanish specifically. The differences aren't great, and for the purpose of brevity, they'll be mostly left out. If you're interested in the version of Spanish spoken in Spain, you'll only have one more verb conjugation to learn and a few different pronunciations. However, your Latin American Spanish will still be understood perfectly overseas should you ever go, you just will sound foreign.

Anyhow, onto pronunciation. Spanish pronunciation has many parallels with English pronunciation, but there are still many caveats that you need to be aware of that set it apart.

Let's start with the vowel sounds. Vowel sounds in English can be a little difficult to understand simply because they can seem pretty all over the place. However, vowel sounds in Spanish are the opposite: they're *extremely* consistent. The vowel sounds in Spanish never, ever change. Bear this in mind as you go forward because this will allow you to read early texts with ease.

The Spanish vowel sounds are as follows:

a	-	ah
e	-	eh
i	-	eeh
o	-	oh
u	-	ooh

As you can see, they're relatively simple, especially compared to the absolute mess that is English vowel sounds. Spanish consonants can be a little tricky but are, for the most part, relatively consistent.

b - b at the beginning of a word, mid-way between English b and v elsewhere

c - makes an English *k* sound unless followed by an *i* or an *e,* in which case, it makes an English *s* sound

ch - makes an English *ch* sound, as in *chair*.

d - there's not a direct corollary in English for the Spanish *d*. It's formed behind the teeth instead of the roof of the mouth and has no air behind it. It sounds almost like *th*.

f	-	makes an English *f* sound.
g	-	makes an English *h* sound.
h	-	always silent! Don't get confused.
j	-	makes an English *h* sound.
k	-	makes an English *k* sound.
l	-	makes an English *l* sound, but produced

with the tongue more forward than in English.

    ll - no English corollary; somewhere between a *y* and a *ch* sound. Just go for the *y* sound and you'll be safe until you're comfortable with the real sound.

m	-	makes an English *m* sound.
n	-	makes an English *n* sound.
ñ	-	makes a sound approximately akin to an

English *ny*.

p	-	makes an English *p* sound.
q	-	makes an English *k* sound, and is

generally followed by a *u*.

    r - three different forms. At beginning of word, it's rolled; in the middle of a word, it's flipped (say *ta-da!* and the *da* sound is an approximation of the *r* sound); at the end of a word, it is rolled.

rr	-	Intense roll!
s	-	makes an English *s* sound.
t	-	much like the *d* sound, there is no

English corollary; you say it like an English *t* but with no air and with the tongue touching the teeth.

v - makes an English *b* sound.

w - makes an English *w* sound; only appears in loanwords.

x - three different sounds depending upon origin. Generally an *ks* sound, like in English, unless it's pulling from an aboriginal word (like *Mexico*) in which case it will be similar to an *h*. In some contexts, it will also be a *ch* sound.

y - Almost always a vowel, pronounced like *eeh*.

z - makes an English *s* sound.

So, there are the essential consonant sounds of Spanish. If you aren't comfortable with them yet, don't worry. You'll become far more comfortable with them as you work with them and branch out in your Spanish speaking. Your mind and tongue simply have to take time to acclimate to them, and that's alright!

There's one last topic that we really have to tackle in terms of pronunciation and that's *accent marks*. Accent marks have a relatively straightforward meaning in Spanish: they indicate which *syllable*, or part of the word, receives the stress. Spanish is a syllable-timed language, which means that when it's spoken, it has a bit of a rhythm to it. These marks will tell you when that rhythm needs to be broken up and you need to put emphasis on a certain part of a word.

The accent marks used in Spanish are all acute accents over the vowel of the syllable: *á, é, í, ó, ú.*

The sound of the syllable and vowel don't change at all; what only changes is the stress of the word, which will be moved to the syllable with the accent mark. This is historically used as a means of telling words that are quite similar apart, as well. For example, compare *si* - meaning *if* - with *sí* - meaning *yes*. The two words are dramatically different, and the accent mark allows you to tell the two apart.

Those are the key aspects of pronunciation in Spanish. Now that we've gotten past that, let's move to another topic: common conversational phrases in Spanish. Particularly common phrases tend to defy traditional grammar, much like in English. This is because they become used very often over the course of a language's development and tend to shorten and consolidate into far shorter phrases.

The first phrases that we need to know are those which are used in order to open *up* a conversation. In English, we'd typically use some variation of "hello" or "good morning" in order to do this.

Here are the different ways to say "hello" in Spanish:

Hola!	Hello!
Buenos días!	Good morning!
Buenas tardes!	Good afternoon!
Buenas noches!	Good evening!
Buenas!	A general greeting, a shortened "good day".

Additionally, in Spain and some regions of Latin America, *Chao* is used quite often as a hello and a goodbye.

The way that you can differentiate between *morning*, *afternoon*, *evening*, and *night* in Spanish is a little arbitrary. The distinction between morning and afternoon occurs, obviously, at noon. The distinction between afternoon and the evening happens a little bit later, generally around 5. The distinction between the evening and the night is simply whenever the sun goes down. If you're in a situation where it's 9 in the evening and the sun is still out, you'll still say *good night*. If you're ever unsure, though, look at the clock; if it's after 8 pm, it's generally a good time to start saying "Buenas noches!".

Goodbyes in Spanish can be a little bit tricky to master. There are a lot of different forms of goodbye. The one we hear most frequently is *adiós*, but the truth is that this one is a bit incorrectly used! Adiós is intended to be more of a permanent send-off; it literally means "Until we meet at God" with the implication being that you won't see one another until you've both died.

The other ways to say goodbye are many. Here are just a few:

Hasta mañana!	See you tomorrow!
Hasta pronto!	See you very soon!
Hasta la vista!	Goodbye, see you around.
Hasta luego!	See you later!
Nos vemos!	We'll meet again.

Again, whichever you use will vary wildly depending upon the circumstances. Their meanings are quite literal and should be taken as such.

You also need to know some basic phrases to keep the conversation going. One thing that you can do is ask how they are or how things are going. There are a lot of ways to do so:

Que tal?	What's up?

Que pasa?   What's happening?
Cómo estás?   How are you? (informal)
Cómo está usted?   How are you? (formal)
Cómo vas?   How's it going? (informal)

We'll get to the difference between the formal and the informal registers in just a moment. For now, the distinction just needs to be made.

There's one more thing to really discuss in this chapter: *verb conjugations*. So, what are verb conjugations?

If you've ever studied another language, you're probably somewhat familiar with what verb conjugations are. After all, most languages in the world have them. Even English has them, though they're just a bit scaled back compared to other languages.

A verb conjugation is a system wherein the ending of a verb is changed in order to reflect the person who is performing or being affected by the verb, depending on the nature of the verb.

As I said, this happens to some degree in English. There are some verb endings in English where we append an *s*. Take a look:

verb: to jump

I jump
You jump
He/she/it jump*s*
We jump
You (all) jump
They jump

Verb conjugation also entails changing the ending of the verb depending upon when the verb is taking place. In English, we can convert something into the past tense by adding an *ed*, generally.

verb: to jump

I jumped
You jumped
He/she/it jumped
We jumped
You (all) jumped
They jumped

These sorts of endings are known as *regular* conjugations. This means that they follow a set system and will never vary from that system. The handy thing about Spanish is that the vast majority of verbs are regular. However, we're not going to be talking about regular verbs in this chapter. We're reserving those for the next chapter as a part of your normal practice that we'll be instituting in week two. This entire first week is simply about memorization of key things.

For that, we're going to focus on irregular verbs. See, the thing about Spanish is that while most verbs *are* regular, none of the most common verbs are. This is simply a result of the fact that the language has been spoken across the vast Spanish empire for several hundreds of years and across various different divided regions of Spain for even longer.

In this chapter, we're going to be covering some of the essential verbs for you to know in your day to day conversations, as well as a few ways that you can use them. With that, we're just going to jump right in.

The first thing that we need to cover about *any* verb is subject pronouns. Subject pronouns are incredibly important. They are one of the defining features of language; they help you define who is speaking and assist you in breaking up the monotony of a text so that it's more approachable and easily understood.

Subject pronouns are any word that replaces the *subject* of the sentence, or the person performing the action. In the sentence "the dog *chases* the ball", the *dog* is the subject because they are the one doing the chasing.

We could replace the word *dog* by using the subject pronoun *It* or, depending on the gender of the dog, *He* or *She*.

In Spanish, there are a few different subject pronouns that you need to be familiar with. They are as follows:

Yo	(I)
Tú	(You)
Él/ella	(He/she)
Usted	(You, formal)
Nosotros	(We)
Ellos/ellas	(They, masculine or mixed; They, feminine)
Ustedes	(You, plural, as in "you all")

Castilian Spanish has another informal plural for you, *vosotros*, but this has been almost entirely dropped in Latin American Spanish and only appears in literature from overseas. Since this adds a whole extra category that you don't really need to learn right now, we're going to leave it out since most places you can speak Spanish won't utilize it anyhow.

With that in mind, we can now move on to conjugating verbs. Verbs are conjugated according to the subject, which means that we can refer to them with the subject pronouns.

Ser   (to be)

Yo	*soy*
Tú	*eres*
Él/ella/usted	*es*
Nosotros	*somos*
Ellos/ellas/ustedes	*son*

Pay attention to the fact that *él, ella,* and *usted,* both in the singular and the plural form, use the same exact conjugation.

There's another verb which means *to be* in Spanish: *estar.* *Estar* is also irregular.

Estar   (to be)
Yo	*estoy*
Tú	*estás*
Él/ella/usted	*está*
Nosotros	*estamos*
Ellos/ellas/ustedes	*están*

You may be wondering, *what's the difference between the two?* Well, the question is a little difficult to answer without context, but it's something you'll largely feel out just by means of experience. The key thing to remember is that *ser* is used for more permanent qualities, like personality traits, hair color, or nationality. *Estar* is used to denote more passing qualities, such as emotions (I *am* happy would be conjugated using estar) and place of being. In this capacity, you can remember the difference between the two largely using the rhyme: "How you feel and where you are, that is when you use *estar*!"

The last irregular verb that we're going to tackle in this chapter is *ir*. *Ir* is a verb which means *to go*. It's conjugated like so:

Ir	(to go)
Yo	*voy*
Tú	*vas*
Él/ella/usted	*va*
Nosotros	*vamos*
Ellos/ellas/ustedes	*van*

This operates much like the verb for *to go* in English. You use it to tell when you're going to go somewhere or when you're going to go do something.

There's one more thing that we need to establish in this chapter: *articles*. There are a few concepts lying behind articles that we have to tackle before going further with the topic, though.

The first is *gender*. Gender is a very important thing in Spanish. Everything has a gender. Note that this doesn't have anything to do with the biological sense of gender. Rather, gender refers to the grammatical gender of a certain object. This harkens back to a concept from the early days of Spanish known as *tone harmony*. Tone harmony is an important concept in Romance languages and is based on the fact that things have to sound right. Spanish is ultimately derived from Latin, which had a *neuter* grammatical gender as well. These three genders, masculine, feminine, and neuter, referred exclusively to the ending of the word and the specific ways of categorizing and utilizing the noun. As Latin developed, this neutral gender was eventually dropped. Since this would eventually grow into modern Romance languages, this had a massive impact on the way that the language would shape up.

Every single noun has a gender, and it has little to do with the noun itself. For example, apples and tables are feminine, but men use these things every day. Meanwhile, trees are masculine, but women walk by them every single day, and there are plenty of female arborists. These distinctions are wholly linguistic, aside from living beings where the ending can be adjusted depending on the gender. For example, *gato*, for cat, can be changed to *gata* to indicate a female cat.

Another important concept is definition. Articles are generally *definite* or *indefinite*. Indefinite refers to any given instance of a noun, and carries the same weight as "a" or "some" in English. Definite refers to a very *specific* instance of a noun, and carries the same weight as "the" in English.

If someone were to say "can you pass me a ball?" in English, you'd not think they were referring to any specific ball. Perhaps there's a basket full of basketballs behind you and you're at a gym, and they're just wanting you to throw them a ball. However, if somebody were to say "can you pass me *the* ball?" in English, they're probably referring to a very specific ball that you're already holding and perhaps even playing with. This distinction is pretty huge.

The last concept that plays into articles is the *plurality*. This goes without saying. If you have more than one of a noun, you're going to need to use plural articles.

Let's use some words that we've already worked with here to

illustrate the concepts. We'll use *manzana*, for apple, and *arbór*, for tree. The first is feminine and the second is masculine.

If we wanted to refer to any given instance of these objects, we'd use an indefinite article. The indefinite articles are like so:

un	arbór	a tree.
una	manzana	an apple.
unos	arbóres	some trees.
unas	manzanas	some apples.

When you want to make something plural in Spanish, you generally just add an *s* unless it ends in a consonant, in which case you add an *es*.

Now, if we wanted to refer to a *specific* instance of these objects, we'd use a *definite* article. These are like so:

el	arbór	the tree.
la	manzana	the apple.
los	arbóres	the trees.
las	manzanas	the apples.

This is the general trend for articles throughout Spanish. It's important that we cover this in chapter one so that you can get some decent coverage on the topic before you go further because if you try to form sentences as you'll be doing in the following chapter, you're going to be lost without this little bit of guidance.

Chapter 3: Days 7-14 - Regular Verbs: Past, Present, and Future

In this chapter, we're going to be talking about regular verbs and the different ways that you can use them. Now, Spanish has several different verb tenses. The ones we're going to be talking about in this chapter are the *present progressive*, the *preterite*, and the *future*. These are all relatively easy to use at their basis. Days seven through fourteen are going to be spent practicing these different verb forms (with an emphasis on the present and present progressive) and doing what you can to get used to regular verb forms and how they work. Acclimating to the verb system is one of the hardest parts of learning a Romance language such as Spanish, but it's not that difficult and I'm confident that with a little elbow grease, you can start to pull it off.

Verbs in Spanish are sorted by their endings. Verb endings in Spanish are called the *stem*; they are the final two letters of the verb. The stems change the way that the verb will conjugate.

When a verb has the stem on it, it's referred to as the *infinitive* form. The infinitive form of the verb is the conceptual form. That is to say that the infinitive form of the verb refers to the verb itself, rather than somebody necessarily performing the verb. In Spanish, the infinitive is formed by way of leaving the *stem* on. In English, we just add the word *to* in front of the verb - "to jump", "to throw", "to run", "to walk".

Spanish verbs are conjugated by removing the stem and then making necessary changes to the verb. These changes involve replacing the stem with another ending.

For present tense verbs, this is pretty simple. Present tense verbs refer to those actions which *do occur*. That is to say, they don't occur in the past and they don't necessarily occur in the future - they occur *at the moment*, even without happening right at the moment. We'll get into that distinction in a moment.

Present tense verbs are incredibly useful. To start forming them, we have to change the stems, as already stated. Spanish verbs have three different stems: *-er*, *-ir*, and *-ar*.

Most Spanish regular verbs end in *-ar*, but plenty of important ones end in *-er* or *-ir*.

Here is how you would conjugate an *-ar* verb. For this example, we're going to use *hablar* meaning *to talk*.

Hablar	(to talk)
Yo	*hablo*
Tú	*hablas*
Él/ella/usted	*habla*
Nosotros	*hablamos*
Ellos/ellas/ustedes	*hablan*

As you can see, all that you do is drop the *-ar* and add a different ending, those endings being respectively -o, -as, -a, -amos, and -an.

In order to form *-er* verbs, you do something similar. Here is how you form a present tense verb with an *-er* stem using the verb *comer*, to eat, as an example.

Comer	(to eat)
Yo	*como*
Tú	*comes*
Él/ella/usted	*come*
Nosotros	*comemos*
Ellos/ellas/ustedes	*comen*

Lastly, come *-ir* verbs. *-ir* verbs are likewise simple, being formed by way of taking the *-ir* off and changing the ending. You'll notice that *-ir* verbs conjugate rather similarly to *-er* verbs, aside from the *nosotros* form. We'll illustrate this using the verb *asistir*, meaning "to attend".

Asistir	(to attend)
Yo	*asisto*
Tú	*asistes*
Él/ella/usted	*asiste*
Nosotros	*asistimos*
Ellos/ellas/ustedes	*asisten*

This is a point at which we should talk about another thing: cognates. Cognates are words which sound like and have the same meaning as their English counterpart. There are many of these in Spanish. However, there are just as many *false cognates* or words which seem like they should share a meaning with an English counterpart but do *not*. Asistir is one of these. At first glance, you'd think that it would share meanings with the English word *assist*, and it would have a meaning similar to "to give aid to"; it does not, however. Be wary of false cognates and if a certain thing doesn't make sense with the context, don't assume that it carries that meaning.

The present progressive is the other present tense in Spanish. This one is different from the present tense because this indicates that something is happening right now. The difference can be illustrated like so: if you're simply learning

Spanish at school and you want to tell somebody that you're learning Spanish, you can say "Aprendo español", which means "I learn Spanish" or "I am learning Spanish". The implication isn't that you're doing it at that exact moment, though. If you wanted to say you were doing something at that exact moment, like you were reading a Spanish book and learning it when somebody asked, you'd use the present progressive.

The present progressive is pretty simple to use. It simply consists of *estar* and the *present participle*. The present participle is pretty straightforward. For regular verbs, all that you do is drop the stem and add *-ando* to *-ar* verbs, or drop the stem and add *-iendo* to regular *-er* and *-ir* verbs.

Let's take *aprender*, to learn. To turn this into the *present participle*, we would simply drop the *-er* and add *-iendo*: *aprendiendo*. Now, let's say that we wanted to say "I am learning Spanish." It would be like so:

- We conjugate *estar* for the subject pronoun *yo*: "estoy"
- We take our verb and convert it to the present participle: *aprender -> aprendiendo*
- We

sandwich them together: *Estoy aprendiendo español.*

At this point, I should note: since the Spanish verb endings are so complex, you generally don't need the subject pronoun in the sentence since it's implied. Often, it's left off entirely. The only time it's really used in conversation is to provide emphasis as to who is performing an action. Instead of *Yo estoy aprendiendo español*, we would just say *estoy aprendiendo español*.

Another major verb tense in Spanish is the *preterite*. The preterite is the basic Spanish past-tense and indicates that something happened finitely in the past.

Let's take the Spanish verb *caminar*, to walk. Let's say that you wanted to say "I walked this morning." To conjugate *caminar*, drop the ending and add the following endings:

Yo caminé
Tú caminaste
El/ella/usted caminó
Nosotros caminamos
Ellos/ellas/ustedes caminaron

So, you would say "Caminé esa mañana."

-er and *-ir* verbs follow a pretty similar conjugation scheme. You just drop the stem and add the following endings - we'll use *vender*, to sell, this time:

*Yo vend*i
*Tú vend*iste
*Él/ella/usted vend*ió
*Nosotros vend*imos
*Ellos/ellas/ustedes vend*ieron

As you can see, forming the Spanish past tense is pretty easy. There's another past tense that we aren't going to get into here, but for the most part, this should be just fine for you.

Now we're moving on to the future tense. Note that for the most part, the future is largely expressed in a combination of the present tense and an expressed time. The future tense is largely used for things that are in the far future.

In order to form the far future, all that you do is take the infinitive, *don't drop the stem this time*, and add one of the following endings. Let's use the verb *beber* meaning *to drink* as an example:

*Yo beber*é
*Tú beber*ás

*Él/ella/usted beber*á
*Nosotros beber*emos
*Ellos/ellas/ustedes beber*án

Again, though, the near future is almost always expressed as the present tense plus a time.

"Voy al cine la noche." - I'm going to the cinema this evening.

With that, we've covered all of the major verb tenses in Spanish or the ones that you'll be using the most. All of this week needs to be spent working with these and learning to use them. Your focus should be spent on the initial two tenses and learning them the best you can. In your free time, also be researching what verbs you can so that you can learn more irregular verbs and more construction. With only thirty minutes per day, by the end of the week, you should feel relatively comfortable with all of these concepts.

Here are some sample verb lists for you to work with.

-Er verbs:

Leer - to read
Comprender - to comprehend

Aprehender - to apprehend
Deber - to must, to should
Conmeter - to commit
Prometer - to promise
Correr - to run
Temer - to break

-Ir verbs:

Abrir - to open
Admitir - to admit
Asistir - to attend
Combatir - to fight
Cumplir - to complete
Escribir - to write
Insistir - to insist
Permitir - to permit
Subir - to climb
Unir - to unite
Vivir - to live

-Ar verbs:

Aceptar - to accept
Bajar - to go down
Bañar - to bathe

Calcular - to calculate

Comparar - to buy

Determinar - to determine

Dictar - to dictate

Envidiar - to envy

Estudiar - to study

Fumar - to smoke

Hablar - to speak

Montar - to ride or mount

Preguntar - to ask

Trabajar - to work

Usar - to use

Viajar - to take a trip

Chapter 4: Days 14-21 - Prepositions, Conjunctions, and Starting a Routine

There are a few different concepts that we need to talk about in this chapter before we go on to the development of a routine.

The first is conjunctions. Conjunctions serve as a way to connect two disjointed concepts. In English, conjunctions are things like *and*, *but*, or *or*. They work exactly the same in Spanish. Here is a list of common Spanish conjunctions:

y	-	and
o	-	or
pero	-	but (familiar)
mas	-	but (academic)
sino	-	rather, instead, but
entonces	-	then, as a result
ni [x] ni [y]	-	neither x nor y
o [x] o [y]	-	either x or y

Next up is prepositions. Prepositions serve as a manner by which you can tell where an object is in relation to others.

a	-	at *or* to
al	-	contraction of *a* and *el*

bajo	-	under
con	-	with
de	-	of *or* from
desde	-	from
en	-	in, on, at
entre	-	between
para	-	for, so that
por	-	for, by, through
sin	-	without
sobre	-	upon, over, above, on

Now that we've finished all of the complex grammatical parts, we can talk about some of the more strenuous parts of this chapter and this technique. By now, you've built up that first level of the pyramid, the foundation. Now, it's time that you start working on the *arbitrations*. The handy thing about this method is that the arbitrations are custom-tailored to suit you and the things that you like. When you care about what you're working with, you're a lot more likely to actually remember and work with it.

This is also going to be the point at which Spanish starts to work its way into your day to day life and have more of a measurable impact than just thirty minutes of practice per day.

In this period, you need to start doing three things.

The first is that you need to start keeping a journal. Every single day, you need to write down at least a paragraph in Spanish about your day. You're going to have a hard time coming up with all of the words that you need. In these cases, it's absolutely fine to use an online dictionary. I prefer WordReference because it has in-depth definitions and is really easy to navigate. Again, at least a paragraph per night about your day. This allows you to solidify the concepts that you already know and work on the ones which you don't know as well.

The second thing that you need to do is find a subject that you really care about. If, for example, you find entrepreneurs really interesting, try to find a Spanish copy of the Steve Jobs biography. Then, every day, work through the biography, translating it into your native language. Do a paragraph per day or thirty minutes per day, whichever comes first. This is going to be extremely hard at first, but it's important. Firstly, it will allow you to start building essential vocabulary skills. Secondly, literature is often professionally translated, which means that even if it wasn't written originally in the target language, it was written by somebody who is very skilled in the target language and most likely didn't make mistakes. Get a notebook and do it by hand so that you can forge those connections even more effectively.

The third thing that you need to do is start utilizing online tools. Make an account on Duolingo and start working through 3 courses every day. Each one should only take five to ten minutes. With the knowledge you've gotten from this book and context clues, you can probably test out of a tier or two as well. Regardless, this will be an important tool as you go on as it will help fill you in on conversational tidbits that you hadn't gathered so far in the book.

Chapter 5: Days 21-30 - Building on Your Routine and Immersion

This is the final part of your thirty-day journey. This is also the hardest part because now that we've learned the foundations from this book, it's completely on *you* to keep going with your education. In the last chapter, we gradually increased your Spanish exposure from 15 to 30 minutes per day to around one to two hours per day, depending on how much you do and how fast you work. This chapter is going to increase your Spanish exposure to being somewhat permanent, which will really be the catalyst to becoming fluent in Spanish. Alongside your other practices, you need to start introducing Spanish everywhere that you can.

For example, when you're watching a movie on Netflix, try turning on Spanish subtitles. Most movies and television shows have them. Perhaps you should try specifically seeking out Spanish television as well, then turning on Spanish subtitles. You may not understand everything, but the context will really help you to solidify the parts of your brain that allow you to pick up language naturally.

You also need to start dedicating more time to the routine that you have. The entire purpose of this period is to start engaging with Spanish as much as possible. Find online communities that speak primarily Spanish and read through the forums; listen to the radio in Spanish; watch Spanish films. Do whatever you can to get as much exposure to this as possible.

It seems rather funny that this is the shortest chapter given that it's the longest period of time, but after a while, there's not much more to do than to practice. I've given you plenty of ideas for how you can immerse yourself in Spanish. The key to this period is simply to actually *do* so. Also, practice the concepts that you've encountered in this book so that you can become more acquainted with things like verb conjugation.

Chapter 6: The Three-Day Masterclass

So now that we've finished the thirty-day track, you may be wondering: how can I learn Spanish in as few as 3 days? Well, that's the purpose of this chapter. We're going to hit the ground running and try to do everything we can to get you adeptly speaking Spanish in very little time. Hopefully, by the end of three days, you'll be relatively fluent in the language.

Now, the thing to remember about this track is that it's *very* intensive. The sad fact is that there is no singular trick to learning a language, especially not one as densely historied as Spanish. It's a long set of work that involves building vocabulary and familiarity. If you want to try to replicate those results in just a few days, the sad fact is that you're going to be spending at least six hours per day - and more likely, something more like eight to nine hours per day - in order to get to a higher level with the language.

If you're willing to put out that much work for quick results, though, this is the track for you. Just remember that Rome wasn't built in a day, and trying to build it in a day will be quite stressful and quite difficult. Only try to do this way if you have the mental fortitude to do so!

Day One:

Now, the hardest thing about this track is that most of this book and this language learning method is built off of steady acquisition by way of immersion. When you're trying to learn a language as rapidly as three days, you have to throw these concepts out of the window when you're starting out because they're *incredibly* effective, but they're relatively slow.

However, regardless of how rapidly you're trying to learn a language, this book still contains a plethora of amazing information for you as a prospective Spanish speaker. The intent was to provide a really firm foundation, and hopefully, that was done. If you've skipped straight ahead to this chapter, then you're going to feel a bit silly.

The objective for you for day one is simply to make your way through this book and then spend a couple hours working with the contents. Conjugate all of the verbs that I've given you and try to really hammer home the regular and irregular verb conjugations. Work with the various different sentence construction and try to even write something of moderate length in Spanish using the content that I've already given you. Once you've worked through the book and done a few hours of exercise, you can call it a day.

This is the most important part because this will give you a stable and well-reasoned foundation with Spanish. This book shouldn't take you more than four hours to read and understand, and then that leaves an hour or two of working with the exercises. That's really a relatively lax first day if you think about it. Regardless of how lax it is, though, the content that you'll learn is still invaluable nonetheless, and having a proper learning experience with this book will set you up for an easy road down the line.

At the end of the day, you should feel like you're at a comfortable level with Spanish, at least. Well enough to make basic conversation and express yourself if handed regular verbs. This is where you want to be. Obviously, you won't be able to do all of the immersion techniques in the book, but you can pick up all of the information regarding the language itself, as there's quite a bit of that.

Day Two:

Day two is going to separate massively from the rest of the book. On day two, you're going to want to start using Duolingo. As ebooks don't necessarily smile on links being included, you'll have to Google it. Duolingo is a free website which can easily be used to learn additional languages - not just Spanish! The trouble with Duolingo is that it doesn't have as much structure as many people would like. That's why this book pairs really well with it; this book will offer the structure that you need in order to really succeed with Duolingo.

At first, a lot of what you learn is going to be rehashing or learning additional vocabulary words. Many things will seem pretty familiar to you early on. The point of Duolingo is to get important experience with listening, speaking, and reading the language. Additionally, it will let you experience more conversational avenues that you haven't experienced here. It will really flesh out your potential conversations and make you feel like you're at a much higher level than you already were.

It also is going to reinforce many of the things that you learned on day one. While this isn't the absolutely perfect way to continue with your learning, it is the best path that I've found for day two of a rigorous Spanish boot camp. The fact that it's designed to be very game-like also makes it somewhat enjoyable to learn on. While it won't be fun after about hour four, it still is a worthwhile pursuit.

You need to do Duolingo for as long as you possibly can. While it's incredibly doubtful that you'll finish the entire course in a single day, you do need to try to finish as much as you can in six to eight hours in order to learn and reinforce as much as possible. It's not a three-day crash course for nothing; you're trying to build up as much skill as you possibly can.

Day Three:

Day three is where you're going to be reinforcing even further everything that you've already learned. Combining the foundational knowledge that you got on day one with the extra knowledge that you built up on day two, you're going to spend day three immersing yourself as much as you can in the language in a real sense. On day three, you should be searching for and reading up on Spanish-language forums. They can be a little difficult to find but, if you look up forums specifically of a certain region, such as Venezuela or Mexico, you can find them with relative ease.

Moreover, if you haven't finished up Duolingo's course, you'll want to do so on this day as well. Really, you need to do everything that you possibly can in order to get your skill up as much as possible on this day, with an emphasis on hearing and seeing the language being used.

When you see a language or hear a language being used by a native speaker and you understand enough to navigate what they're saying, you subconsciously start to pick up the language patterns that you need in order to sound like a native speaker yourself. You'll pick up little nuances of the language subconsciously that you may not otherwise.

The people who spend a fair amount of time learning a language properly and listening to native speakers speak the language are generally those who understand the caveats of a language best and know the language the best themselves.

You can take some nods from some of the earlier chapters in this book, but they may not be particularly effective in this setting. For example, though, you can watch Spanish television with English subtitles and let your ears do all of the work.

You also should spend some time on this day poking around Spanish literature. If you're in America, there should be a mercado relatively close to you where you can find magazines that are aimed at Hispanics. There, you'll find rather formal Spanish that doesn't suffer from any of the ailments that can happen with less formal writing.

Day three is completely based on reinforcement and comfortability. The first two days were intended to build structure and vocabulary; this day is simply intended to reinforce what you've already learned. Don't stress too much about learning new words; at this point, your brain should be doing so somewhat naturally.

Spend as much time as you can, doing this. Again, you'll need six to eight hours of practice at the very least in order to solidify all of the concepts.

Reflection:

On day four, the most important part comes into play: continuing to use what you've learned. It's likely that your brain will be pretty drained on Spanish learning at this point, but you have to have the discipline to continue working with Spanish for at least an hour every day and using Spanish media when you can. As the other chapters in this book point out, you need to try to learn things and do things that you enjoy *in Spanish*. This way, your brain starts to naturally soak up the language as you navigate the things that you do and don't already know.

Conclusion

Thank for making it through to the end of *Learning Spanish Can Be Fun*, let's hope it was informative and able to provide you with all of the tools you need to achieve your goals whatever it may be.

The next step is to take off the training wheels. Whether you took the 30-day or the 3-day course from this book, you need to remove the various things that are acting as crutches, because you should now be comfortable enough in the language to get around in it on your own. There are many different things in this book that help you hold yourself up on the Spanish bicycle, such as the subtitles for the Spanish television or the translation of Spanish works into your native language, but you have to eventually take those off.

Here's why: you are *never* going to be fluent if you always rely on your native tongue. You have to turn on the period of your brain that has to make an effort in the language to truly be effective in it. Otherwise, you aren't going to gain much of anything. You're always going to be internally translating from English to Spanish if you never make yourself quit, and that's not a good way to sound like a native speaker. Your conversations will be slow and you'll never truly internalize the nuances of the language the way that you're wanting to.

You also need to accept that you are going to make mistakes and speak to Spanish speakers. I can't stress this enough. You learn a language best when you speak to those who actually know the language by heart (and by mind). You are *not* going to speak Spanish perfectly. Chances are that you don't even speak English perfectly, but you simply aren't self-conscious about it because it's your native tongue. Don't be self-conscious about speaking Spanish either. All that is going to do is ultimately hold you back, and that's the last thing that you need in your development as a language learner.

Learning a language is hard and is many times a labor of love. In fact, there will be many times where you feel completely lost. It's through perseverance and hard work that you're going to become a really effective Spanish speaker.

So with that, I wish you the best of luck, and I hope that I've been instrumental in helping you develop a foundation for Spanish speaking.

www.ingramcontent.com/pod-product-compliance
Lightning Source LLC
LaVergne TN
LVHW010435070526
838199LV00066B/6029